LE CORDON BLEU

HOME COLLECTION

QUICHES & PASTRIES

MEREHURST

contents

recipe ratings ✹ *easy* ✹✹ *a little more care needed* ✹✹✹ *more care needed*

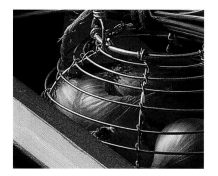

Salmon millefeuilles

A delicious savoury variation of the classic French millefeuille, this dish is made with layers of light flaky pastry, lightly cooked salmon and a mouthwatering chive butter sauce.

*Preparation time **1 hour + 15 minutes chilling***
*Total cooking time **1 hour 30 minutes***
Serves 4

400 g (12³/₄ oz) salmon fillet, skinned and deboned
2 tablespoons olive oil
¹/₂ quantity puff pastry (see page 60)
1 egg, beaten
4 sprigs fresh chervil, to garnish

SAUCE
2 French shallots, finely chopped
250 ml (8 fl oz) white wine
1 tablespoon white wine vinegar
60 ml (2 fl oz) thick (double) cream
200 g (6¹/₂ oz) unsalted butter, chilled and cubed
2 tablespoons chopped fresh chives

1 Cut the salmon into 24 thin slices, about 5 mm (¹/₄ inch) thick. Season with salt and pepper, and drizzle with the olive oil. Cover and set aside. Lightly grease a baking tray and line with baking paper.
2 Preheat the oven to hot 210°C (415°F/Gas 6–7). Divide the puff pastry in half, and roll each half out on a lightly floured surface to a 29 x 25 cm (11¹/₂ x 10 inch) rectangle, 3 mm (¹/₈ inch) thick. Prick all over with a fork and refrigerate for 15 minutes. Place one half of the pastry on the baking tray, and cover with a sheet of baking paper and a second baking tray. Bake for 10–15 minutes, then flip the pastry and the trays over and bake for 10 minutes, or until the pastry is lightly golden and evenly coloured. Lightly brush with the beaten egg. Bake, uncovered, for 3–4 minutes, or until glossy. Place on a wire rack to cool slightly, then repeat with the other half of pastry. Cut each sheet of pastry into four 9 cm (3¹/₂ inch) squares.
3 To make the sauce, place the shallots in a saucepan with the white wine and vinegar, and bring to the boil over medium heat. Cook until the liquid has almost completely evaporated, about 15–20 minutes. Add the cream and cook for a further 2–3 minutes. Whisk in the butter, a few pieces at a time, mixing well after each addition. Season to taste with salt and white pepper.
4 Heat a little olive oil in a frying pan over high heat. Cook the salmon slices in batches for about 10 seconds on each side, turning gently. Set aside.
5 Place a square of pastry in the centre of each plate. Arrange six slices of salmon on top and cover with a second square of pastry. Whisk the chives into the warm sauce, and drizzle around the base of each millefeuille. Top each with a sprig of chervil, and serve immediately.

Wild mushroom quiche

This quiche may be made with any combination of wild and button mushrooms, depending on what is available. Wild mushrooms have a strong flavour so the proportion of these to the mild-flavoured button mushrooms should be adjusted according to personal preference.

*Preparation time **45 minutes***
*Total cooking time **1 hour 10 minutes***
Serves 4–6

✵

1/2 quantity shortcrust pastry (see page 58)
1 egg, beaten

FILLING
60 g (2 oz) unsalted butter
400 g (123/4 oz) chanterelles, ceps (porcini), shiitake, oyster, button mushrooms or any combination of the above, sliced
2 French shallots, finely chopped
1 egg
2 egg yolks
100 ml (31/4 fl oz) thick (double) cream
1 tablespoon each of chopped fresh chives, parsley and chervil

1 Lightly grease a 20.5 x 2.5 cm (81/4 x 1 inch) loose-bottomed flan tin. Roll out the pastry on a lightly floured surface to a thickness of 3 mm (1/8 inch) and line the prepared tin (see Chef's techniques, page 59). Preheat the oven to moderate 180°C (350°F/Gas 4). Bake blind for 25 minutes, or until firm. Remove the beans and paper, and brush the bottom of the pastry with the beaten egg. Bake for a further 7 minutes (see Chef's techniques, page 59).

2 To make the filling, melt the butter in a non-stick frying pan over medium-high heat. Sauté the mushrooms for about 5 minutes, or until all their water has evaporated. (If using more than one type of mushroom, sauté each separately.) Add the chopped shallots and cook for 1 minute, then strain and set aside to cool.

3 Whisk the egg, egg yolks, cream and herbs. Season to taste with salt and pepper.

4 Spread the mushroom mixture over the bottom of the cooked pastry shell. Pour in the egg mixture, and bake for 25–30 minutes, or until the mixture has set and a knife inserted into the centre comes out clean. Set on a wire rack to cool slightly before removing from the tin. Leave for 5 minutes before cutting.

Gougères

In Burgundy these cheese-flavoured choux pastry puffs are traditionally served cold with wine during tastings in cellars. On page 62 there are step-by-step illustrations to accompany this recipe.

Preparation time **25 minutes**
Total cooking time **25 minutes**
Makes 25–30

65 g (2¼ oz) plain flour
30 g (1 oz) unsalted butter
pinch of nutmeg
2 eggs
40 g (1¼ oz) Gruyère or Cheddar cheese, finely grated
1 egg, beaten

1 Preheat the oven to warm 170°C (325°F/Gas 3). Lightly grease two baking trays. Sift the flour onto a sheet of greaseproof paper. Place 125 ml (4 fl oz) water in a saucepan with the butter, nutmeg and a pinch of salt. Heat until the butter and water come to the boil. Remove from the heat and add the flour all at once. Mix well using a wooden spoon. Return to the heat and mix until a smooth ball forms and the paste leaves the sides of the pan. Remove from the heat and place the paste in a bowl. Lightly beat the eggs in a small bowl. Using a wooden spoon or electric beaters, add the eggs to the paste a little at a time, beating well after each addition. The mixture is ready when it is smooth, thick and glossy. Mix in half the cheese.

2 Spoon the mixture into a piping bag fitted with a small plain nozzle. Pipe out 2.5 cm (1 inch) balls of dough onto the prepared trays, leaving a space of 3 cm (1¼ inches) between each ball. Using a fork dipped in the beaten egg, slightly flatten the top of each ball. Sprinkle with the remaining grated cheese. Bake for 20–25 minutes, or until the balls have puffed up and are golden brown. Serve hot.

Chef's tip This is a very simple and light finger food to serve with pre-dinner drinks. Gougères are sometimes served in restaurants with drinks and referred to as 'amuse-bouche', the French term for appetizer.

Provençal tart

Bursting with the flavours of the south of France, the filling for this yeast-dough tart consists of onion, garlic, tomato, zucchini and eggplant, cooked in olive oil and lightly flavoured with fresh basil.

Preparation time **1 hour 15 minutes**
     + 40 minutes proving
Total cooking time **1 hour**
Serves **4–6**

PASTRY
200 g (6¹/2 oz) plain flour
I teaspoon salt
I teaspoon caster sugar
10 g (¹/4 oz) fresh yeast or 5 g (¹/8 oz) dried yeast
I egg
2 tablespoons olive oil

FILLING
olive oil, for cooking
I small onion, diced
pinch of salt
200 g (6¹/2 oz) tomatoes, peeled, seeded and chopped (see page 63)
2 cloves garlic, finely chopped
I zucchini (courgette), diced
I eggplant (aubergine), diced
I egg
I egg yolk
100 ml (3¹/4 fl oz) cream
2 tablespoons chopped fresh basil

1 To make the pastry, sift together the flour, salt and sugar into a large bowl. Make a well in the centre. In a bowl, dissolve the yeast in 60 ml (2 fl oz) warm water. Whisk in the egg and olive oil, pour into the well and gradually mix in the flour mixture using a wooden spoon. Once a rough dough has formed, turn it out onto a floured work surface, scraping the bowl out if necessary. Knead the dough for about 5 minutes, or until it is smooth and it no longer sticks to the surface. Lightly brush a bowl with oil and place the dough inside. Cover with an oiled piece of plastic wrap and set aside to rise in a warm place for about 30–40 minutes, or until it is doubled in volume.

2 To make the filling, heat a little olive oil in a deep frying pan. Add the onion and salt, and cook over medium heat for 3–5 minutes, or until soft, without browning the onion. Add the tomato and garlic, and continue to cook over low heat, stirring occasionally, for about 3 minutes, or until the liquid evaporates. Sauté the zucchini and eggplant separately in some olive oil. Add to the tomato mixture, cover and cook over low heat for 15 minutes. Season to taste with salt and pepper, and transfer to a bowl set in ice. Leave to cool, stirring from time to time.

3 Preheat the oven to warm 170°C (325°F/Gas 3). Lightly grease a 20.5 x 2.5 cm (8¹/4 x 1 inch) loose-bottomed flan tin. Whisk together the egg, egg yolk and cream in a small bowl. Season with salt and pepper.

4 Punch the dough down and turn out onto a floured work surface. Lightly dust with flour, roll out to a 3 mm (¹/8 inch) thickness and line the prepared tin (see Chef's techniques, page 59). Cover with a damp tea towel and set aside.

5 Mix the egg mixture and chopped basil into the cool vegetables. Pour into the pastry shell and bake for 30–35 minutes, or until the pastry is nicely coloured. Set on a wire rack to cool slightly before removing from the tin. Leave for 5 minutes before cutting.

Sun-dried tomato twists

These light, tomato-flavoured twists are excellent served either cold or warm. Perfect to serve with drinks, they may be prepared well in advance and stored in an airtight container.

Preparation time **20 minutes**
    + 1 hour 15 minutes chilling
Total cooking time **15 minutes**
Makes about 80

250 g (8 oz) plain flour
1/2 teaspoon salt
pinch of pepper
pinch of paprika
1/2 teaspoon baking powder
150 g (5 oz) unsalted butter, chilled and cubed
dash of Tabasco
4 tablespoons chopped fresh chives
1 egg, lightly beaten
100 g (31/4 oz) tomato paste
50 g (13/4 oz) sun-dried tomatoes, finely chopped

1 Grease two baking trays. Sift the flour into a bowl with the salt, pepper, paprika and baking powder. Add the butter and Tabasco, and rub into the flour until the mixture resembles fine breadcrumbs. Stir in the chives and make a well in the centre.

2 Lightly whisk the egg in a small bowl, pour half into a bowl with half of the tomato paste, and discard the remaining egg. Using a flat-bladed knife, stir into the flour mixture in a circular motion until combined. Gather together into a rough ball of dough. Wrap in plastic wrap and refrigerate for 1 hour.

3 Roll out the dough on a lightly floured surface to a thickness of 3 mm (1/8 inch). Place on a clean tray, cover with plastic wrap and refrigerate for 15 minutes.

4 Preheat the oven to moderately hot 200°C (400°F/ Gas 6). Place the remaining tomato paste and the sun-dried tomatoes in a food processor or blender, and process to a smooth paste. Spread over the pastry, cut into 1 cm (1/2 inch) wide strips and twist evenly.

5 Place the twists on the prepared baking trays, giving each one a twist as you place it on the tray. Press the ends onto the tray to prevent them from unwinding. Bake for 10–15 minutes, or until golden brown and firm to the touch. Cut the twists into 7 cm (23/4 inch) lengths while still hot. Transfer to a wire rack to cool before serving.

Spinach and ricotta quiche

*The classic combination of spinach and ricotta cheese, subtly enhanced with the flavour
of nutmeg, makes a delicious filling for this vegetarian quiche.*

*Preparation time **30 minutes***
*Total cooking time **1 hour 10 minutes***
Serves 4–6

FILLING
500 g (1 lb) English spinach
20 g (³/4 oz) unsalted butter
3 eggs
200 g (6¹/2 oz) ricotta cheese
100 ml (3¹/4 fl oz) thick (double) cream
nutmeg, to taste

¹/2 quantity shortcrust pastry (see page 58)
I egg, beaten

1 To make the filling, wash the spinach well, remove
the stems and pat dry with paper towels. Melt the
butter in a deep frying pan over medium heat. Add the
spinach and cook for about 8 minutes, or until it is
wilted and the water has evaporated. Place in a strainer
to cool, squeeze out any excess liquid and then finely
chop the spinach.

2 Preheat the oven to moderate 180°C (350°F/Gas 4).
Lightly grease a 20.5 x 2.5 cm (8¹/4 x 1 inch) loose-
bottomed flan tin. Roll out the pastry on a lightly
floured surface to a thickness of 3 mm (¹/8 inch) and
line the prepared tin (see Chef's techniques, page 59).
Bake blind for about 25 minutes, or until firm. Remove
the beans and paper, and brush the bottom of the pastry
with the beaten egg. Bake for another 7 minutes (see
Chef's techniques, page 59).

3 Whisk the eggs, cheese and cream in a bowl, and add
the spinach. Season with salt, pepper and nutmeg. Pour
into the pastry and bake for 25–30 minutes, or until set
and a knife inserted into the centre comes out clean. Set
on a wire rack to cool slightly before removing from the
tin. Leave for 5 minutes before cutting.

Leek tartlets

These small tartlets filled with leek and cumin are ideal served warm with drinks. Alternatively they could be made as larger tarts and served as a first course.

*Preparation time **45 minutes + 15 minutes chilling***
*Total cooking time **40 minutes***
Makes 30

FILLING
40 g (1¼ oz) unsalted butter
1 large leek, white part only, thinly sliced
  (see page 63)
1 bay leaf
pinch of dried thyme
pinch of salt
¼ teaspoon ground cumin
160 ml (5¼ fl oz) thick (double) cream
1 egg
1 egg yolk

1 quantity shortcrust pastry (see page 58)

1 To make the filling, melt the butter in a saucepan over low heat. Add the leek, bay leaf, thyme and salt. Cover and cook slowly for 5 minutes, then uncover and continue cooking for about 5–10 minutes, or until the mixture is dry. Remove the bay leaf. Add the cumin, mix well and set aside to cool.

2 Grease three 12-hole (30 ml/1 fl oz capacity) mini muffin tins or patty pans. Roll out the pastry on a lightly floured surface to a thickness of 3 mm (1/8 inch), and refrigerate for 5 minutes. Preheat the oven to warm 170°C (325°F/Gas 3). Using a 7 cm (2¾ inch) plain round cutter, cut out 30 rounds from the pastry. Press the rounds into the prepared muffin tins or patty pans, pressing well along the bottoms so the dough extends slightly above the edge of the tins. Refrigerate the lined tins for 10 minutes.

3 Whisk together the cream, egg and egg yolk, and season with salt and pepper. Fill each tartlet shell with ½ teaspoon of the leek mixture, then carefully pour in the cream mixture. Bake for 10–15 minutes, or until the filling is set. Remove the tartlets from the tins while still warm. If they stick, loosen them carefully with the tip of a small knife.

Salmon and basil flan

A delicately flavoured flan, excellent served as a light lunch on a hot summer's day with a crisp green salad and a glass of chilled dry white wine.

Preparation time **40 minutes**
Total cooking time **1 hour**
Serves **4–6**

¹/₂ quantity shortcrust pastry (see page 58)
I egg, beaten

FILLING
300 g (10 oz) fresh salmon, skinned and deboned
I egg
150 ml (5 fl oz) thick (double) cream
200 ml (6¹/₂ fl oz) milk
I tablespoon finely chopped fresh basil

1 Preheat the oven to moderate 180°C (350°F/Gas 4). Lightly grease a 22 x 2.5 cm (8³/4 x 1 inch) loose-bottomed flan tin. Roll out the pastry on a lightly floured surface to a thickness of 3 mm (1/8 inch) and line the prepared tin (see Chef's techniques, page 59).

Bake blind for about 25 minutes, or until firm. Remove the beans and paper, and brush the bottom of the pastry with the beaten egg. Bake for another 7 minutes (see Chef's techniques, page 59).

2 To make the filling, cut the salmon into small cubes. Place in a food processor and process in short bursts until finely chopped. Add the egg and process for 10 seconds, then add the cream and process until smooth. Transfer to a mixing bowl and whisk in the milk. Season with salt and pepper and stir in the basil.

3 Pour the mixture into the pastry shell, and bake for 20–30 minutes, or until the flan is set. The tip of a knife inserted into the centre should come out clean. Set on a wire rack to cool slightly before removing from the tin. Allow the flan to cool slightly before serving. Serve warm with a green salad.

Chef's tip Crumbled pieces of poached salmon or chopped smoked salmon may be sprinkled over the bottom before the flan is filled.

Creamy ham tart

Slices of ham in a creamy white sauce, topped with golden-brown melted cheese make this a popular tart with adults and children alike. A variation of this recipe could be made by using smoked ham or by adding a little Dijon mustard to the sauce.

*Preparation time **30 minutes + 20 minutes cooling***
*Total cooking time **45 minutes***
Serves 4–6

❖

1/2 quantity shortcrust pastry (see page 58)

FILLING
60 g (2 oz) unsalted butter
60 g (2 oz) plain flour
500 ml (16 fl oz) milk
150 g (5 oz) ham, cut into 4 x 1 cm
   (1 1/2 x 1/2 inch) strips
pinch of nutmeg
80 g (2 3/4 oz) Emmenthal cheese, grated or
   thinly sliced

1 Preheat the oven to moderate 180°C (350°F/Gas 4). Grease an 18.5 x 2.5 cm (7 1/4 x 1 inch) loose-bottomed flan tin. Roll out the pastry on a lightly floured surface to a circle approximately 3–5 mm (1/8–1/4 inch) thick, and line the prepared tin (see Chef's techniques, page 59).

2 Bake blind for 10 minutes, or until firm. Remove the beans and paper, and bake for another 5 minutes, or until the centre begins to colour (see Chef's techniques, page 59). Remove from the oven to cool and reduce the temperature to warm 170°C (325°F/Gas 3).

3 To make the filling, melt the butter in a heavy-based pan over medium heat. Sprinkle the flour over the base of the pan and cook for 1–2 minutes without colouring, stirring continuously with a wooden spoon. Gradually add the milk to the flour mixture, whisking vigorously to avoid lumps. Be careful not to splash the milk. Stir continuously over medium heat, bubbling, for about 8 minutes, or until the sauce is thick and creamy and is reduced by about two thirds. When a spoon is drawn across the base of the pan, the base should be clearly seen. Stir in the ham and nutmeg, and season with salt and pepper. Cover the surface with baking paper, and set aside to cool for 20 minutes.

4 Spread the mixture into the pastry. Sprinkle the cheese on top and bake for about 10–15 minutes, or until the cheese is golden and bubbling. For added colour, finish the tart by setting under a hot grill for about 30 seconds. Set on a wire rack to cool slightly before removing from the tin. Leave for 15–20 minutes to set before cutting into wedges. Serve warm.

Three-capsicum quiche

Both colourful and tasty, this quiche is best served warm. If yellow capiscum is not available, use red and green only, bearing in mind that the red capiscum has a much softer, sweeter flavour than the green.

Preparation time **45 minutes**
Total cooking time **1 hour 35 minutes**
Serves **4–6**

FILLING
I red capsicum (pepper)
I yellow capsicum (pepper)
I green capsicum (pepper)
3 eggs
250 ml (8 fl oz) thick (double) cream
nutmeg, to taste
40 g (I¹/4 oz) Gruyère cheese, grated

¹/2 quantity shortcrust pastry (see page 58)
I egg, beaten

1 To make the filling, grill the capsicums following the method in the Chef's techniques on page 63, then slice the flesh lengthways into strips.

2 Preheat the oven to warm 170°C (325°F/Gas 3). Lightly grease a 22 x 3.5 cm (8³/4 x 1¹/4 inch) loose-bottomed flan tin. Roll out the pastry on a lightly floured surface to a thickness of 3 mm (¹/8 inch) and line the prepared tin (see Chef's techniques, page 59). Bake blind for about 25 minutes, or until firm. Remove the beans and paper, and brush the bottom of the pastry with the beaten egg. Bake for another 7 minutes (see Chef's techniques, page 59).

3 Whisk together the eggs and cream, and season to taste with salt, pepper and nutmeg. Spread the capsicum over the bottom of the cooked pastry shell and then sprinkle with the grated cheese. Pour in the egg mixture and bake for 40 minutes, or until the mixture has set and a knife inserted into the centre comes out clean. Set on a wire rack to cool slightly before removing from the tin. Leave the quiche to set for 5 minutes before cutting.

Prawn bouchées

Bouchées are small round cases of puff pastry with a tasty filling. These were fashionable at the court of Louis XV of France and his wife, renowned for her hearty appetite.

Preparation time **15 minutes + 35 minutes chilling**
Total cooking time **20 minutes**
Makes 8

1/2 quantity puff pastry (see page 60)
I egg, beaten

FILLING
30 g (I oz) unsalted butter
30 g (I oz) plain flour
250 ml (8 fl oz) fish or shellfish stock, or milk
250 g (8 oz) cooked shelled prawns
2 tablespoons chopped mixed fresh herbs

1 Brush a large baking tray with butter, and refrigerate until needed. Roll out the pastry on a lightly floured surface to a 5 mm (1/4 inch) thickness. Brush off any excess flour from the surface and cut out eight circles with a 7 cm (2³/4 inch) fluted round cutter. Sprinkle the prepared tray with a little cold water, turn the circles over and place on the tray. Brush with the egg, chill for 5 minutes, then brush again. Using a floured 5 cm (2 inch) plain round cutter, press into the pastry three quarters of the way through to mark an inner circle. Refrigerate for 30 minutes.

2 Preheat the oven to hot 220°C (425°F/Gas 7). Brush the top of each pastry circle again with beaten egg. Bake on the middle shelf of the oven for 10–12 minutes, or until the pastry circles are well risen, crisp and golden. Remove from the oven and cut around the centre circle to remove the lid while still warm. Scrape out the excess soft pastry from inside the little cases. If you wish, return to the oven for 30 seconds to dry. (You may turn the oven off and use its residual heat to do this.)

3 To make the filling, melt the butter in a pan, add the flour and cook over low heat for 1 minute. Remove from the heat and pour in the stock or milk, blend thoroughly with a wooden spoon and return to the stove. Stir continuously over low heat until the mixture is free of lumps. Increase the heat and stir until the mixture boils, then simmer for 2–3 minutes. Just before serving, stir in the prawns to warm through. Finally add the herbs and season to taste with salt and pepper.

4 Spoon the filling into the pastry cases while both are still warm. If you wish, garnish with chopped herbs or extra prawns. You may replace the lid or not.

Chef's tips If using frozen cooked prawns, they must be well thawed and drained. Do not wash them, or thaw in cold water, as they will lose a lot of flavour.

After cutting out the pastry circles, they are turned over on the tray to help them to rise with straight sides.

If the cooked cases are left to cool, reheat in a moderate 180°C (350°F/Gas 4) oven for 5 minutes and fill with the hot filling.

Potato and bacon tart

This delicious tart is made of shortcrust pastry topped with thinly sliced potato, bacon, cheese, parsley and a creamy filling, and is best served warm. It is important to slice the potatoes thinly to ensure that they cook completely.

Preparation time **25 minutes**
Total cooking time **1 hour**
Serves 6

1/2 quantity shortcrust pastry (see page 58)

FILLING
1 potato, finely sliced
100 g (3¹/4 oz) bacon, cut into strips
  1 cm (¹/2 inch) wide
2 eggs
120 ml (4 fl oz) thick (double) cream
100 ml (3¹/4 fl oz) milk
1 teaspoon finely chopped fresh parsley
50 g (1³/4 oz) Emmenthal cheese, grated

1 Preheat the oven to moderate 180°C (350°F/Gas 4). Grease a 19 x 27 x 2.5 cm (7¹/2 x 10³/4 x 1 inch) rectangular loose-bottomed flan tin. Roll out the pastry on a floured surface to approximately 3 mm (¹/8 inch) in thickness and line the prepared tin (see Chef's techniques, page 59).

2 Bake blind for 10 minutes, or until firm. Remove the beans and paper, and bake for another 5 minutes, or until the centre begins to colour (see Chef's techniques, page 59). Remove from the oven to cool and reduce the temperature to warm 170°C (325°F/Gas 3).

3 To make the filling, pat the potato slices dry with paper towels. Put the bacon in a small pan, cover with cold water, bring to the boil and cook for 2 minutes, then drain. Mix the eggs, cream and milk together in a small bowl, and season with salt and pepper.

4 Arrange the potato slices and bacon evenly on the bottom of the pastry shell, and sprinkle the parsley and cheese over the top. Pour in the egg mixture and bake for 35–45 minutes, or until the tart is set, the surface is golden and bubbly, and the potatoes are cooked. (Test by inserting the tip of a knife to check that the potatoes are tender.) Set on a wire rack to cool slightly before removing from the tin. Serve the tart warm with a crisp green salad.

Sausage rolls

Versatile, crisp, golden puff pastry filled with well-seasoned sausage mince. Sausage rolls are a light luncheon or picnic dish with salad or a lunch-box standby. Mini sausage rolls would make elegant cocktail savouries for special occasions.

Preparation time **15 minutes + 15 minutes chilling**
Total cooking time **25 minutes**
Makes 8

❁

10 g (¹/4 oz) unsalted butter
2 French shallots, finely chopped
250 g (8 oz) sausage mince
pinch of mixed spice
1 tablespoon finely chopped fresh parsley
1 quantity puff pastry (see page 60)
1 egg, beaten with a pinch of salt

1 Melt the butter in a frying pan and add the shallots. Cover and cook over moderate heat for 5 minutes, or until softened. Remove from the pan and allow to cool for 5 minutes. Put the sausage mince in a bowl and add the shallots, mixed spice and parsley. Season with salt and pepper, and mix well. Roll the sausage mince out with well-floured palms on a well-floured surface to a long rope 2.5 cm (1 inch) thick. Transfer to a lightly floured tray and chill while the pastry is being prepared.

2 Roll the pastry on a lightly floured surface to a long rectangle 3 mm (¹/8 inch) thick and at least 10 cm (4 inches) wide. Trim the edges to neaten. Lay the rope of sausage mince down the length of the pastry to one side of the centre, and trim off the excess pastry at the two ends. Brush the smaller width of visible pastry next to the sausage mince with beaten egg, and fold the larger piece of pastry over the sausage mince to enclose it. Lightly press together the two pastry edges to seal. Trim the edges to neaten. With a lightly floured, thin sharp knife, cut into eight individual sausage rolls. Make three diagonal slits on top of each roll through to the meat to decorate, but also to allow the excess steam to escape. Place on a baking tray that has been lightly dampened with cold water. Brush with beaten egg, avoiding the open cut edges or they will seal during baking and prevent the pastry from rising. Refrigerate for 15 minutes.

3 Preheat the oven to hot 220°C (425°F/Gas 7). Brush the pastry again with the beaten egg and bake in the top half of the oven for about 25 minutes, or until well risen, crisp and golden brown. Serve hot or cold.

Chef's tips Make mini sausage rolls for serving with cocktails or try interesting variations to the filling by adding herbs or chopped sun-dried tomatoes to the sausage mince.

For another variation, hard boil and shell quail eggs. Flatten the sausage meat and arrange the eggs in a line down the centre. Fold and shape the sausage mince around them.

The bases of these sausage rolls will be dark brown.

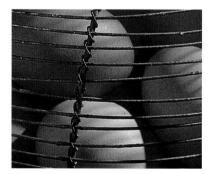

Quiche lorraine

This open tart originated in the Lorraine region around the sixteenth century. The name quiche comes from the German word 'küchen', meaning cake. A quiche can contain many fillings, but a quiche lorraine is traditionally made with cream, eggs and smoked bacon, and is considered a classic of French cuisine.

Preparation time **30 minutes**
Total cooking time **1 hour 5 minutes**
Serves 4–6

1/2 quantity shortcrust pastry (see page 58)
1 egg, beaten

FILLING
oil, for cooking
180 g (5³/4 oz) smoked bacon, rind removed
  and cut into thin strips
3 eggs
nutmeg, to taste
250 ml (8 fl oz) cream
80 g (2³/4 oz) Gruyère cheese,
  grated

1 Lightly grease a 22 x 3.5 cm (8³/4 x 1¹/4 inch) loose-bottomed flan tin. Roll out the dough on a lightly floured surface to a thickness of 3 mm (¹/8 inch) and line the prepared tin (see Chef's techniques, page 59). Preheat the oven to moderate 180°C (350°F/Gas 4). Bake blind for about 25 minutes, or until firm. Remove the beans and paper, and brush the bottom of the pastry with the beaten egg. Bake for another 7 minutes (see Chef's techniques, page 59).

2 To make the filling, heat a little oil in a frying pan. Sauté the bacon, drain on paper towels and set aside. Whisk the eggs with the nutmeg, and season with salt and pepper. Mix in the cream and strain through a sieve.

3 Sprinkle the bottom of the pastry with the bacon and cheese. Gently pour in the egg mixture until the pastry is three-quarters full. Bake for about 20–30 minutes, or until the filling is well coloured and is set. Serve hot.

Cheese palmiers and straws

These small savouries are delicious served with a cocktail or to accompany a soup. They can either be made as palmiers or as cheese straws, and flavoured with herbs, sun-dried tomatoes or anchovy.

Preparation time 30 minutes + 45 minutes chilling
Total cooking time 10 minutes
Makes 30 palmiers or 45 cheese straws

2 egg yolks
I egg
1/4 teaspoon caster sugar
40 g (1 1/4 oz) Parmesan, grated
1/4 teaspoon paprika
I quantity puff pastry (see page 60)

1 Beat together the egg yolks, egg, sugar and 1/4 teaspoon salt, and strain into a clean bowl.

2 Grease a large baking tray with melted butter, and refrigerate until needed. In a small bowl, mix together the Parmesan, paprika and 1/4 teaspoon salt, and season with freshly ground black pepper.

3 Roll out the pastry on a lightly floured surface to a 20 x 24 cm (8 x 9 1/2 inch) rectangle, 3 mm (1/8 inch) thick. Brush lightly with the egg mixture and sprinkle evenly with the Parmesan mixture. Roll again to a 2 mm (1/8 inch) thickness to press the cheese into the pastry. Carefully slide the pastry onto a tray and refrigerate for 15 minutes. Transfer the pastry to a lightly floured surface and trim to a 30 x 15 cm (12 x 6 inch) rectangle.

4 To make the cheese palmiers, lightly mark six 5 cm (2 inch) strips with the back of a knife, parallel with the shortest side. Do not cut, only mark as a guide. Sprinkle lightly with water.

5 Fold the two outer strips flat inwards. Their non-cheese undersides will now be on top—brush them with a little water and fold over onto the next marked sixths, brush again and fold onto each other. Transfer to a tray and refrigerate for 15 minutes. Cut into 5 mm (1/4 inch) slices and place cut-side-down, well apart, on the prepared baking tray. Press them down lightly with the palm of your hand to flatten them, turn them over and refrigerate for 15 minutes.

6 Meanwhile, preheat the oven to moderately hot 200°C (400°F/Gas 6). Bake the palmiers for about 10 minutes, or until golden and crisp. Immediately remove from the tray onto a wire rack to cool.

7 To make the cheese straws, follow steps 1–3. Using a large sharp knife, cut the pastry lengthwise into 1 cm (1/2 inch) wide strips and twist each strip several times to form one long, even, loose ringlet. Place on a baking tray and press both ends down firmly to stop the strip unravelling as it bakes. Refrigerate for 10–15 minutes. Meanwhile, preheat the oven to moderately hot 200°C (400°F/Gas 6). Bake for 7–10 minutes, or until golden brown and crisp. Immediately cut each straw into 10 cm (4 inch) lengths and transfer to a wire rack to cool.

Chef's tip Add some dried mixed herbs to the cheese, or try a little finely chopped sun-dried tomato or anchovy.

Spinach and Brie flan

Creamy Brie cheese is combined with onion, spinach and tomato for the filling of this puff-pastry flan.
It is best served warm with a tomato or crisp green salad.

Preparation time 25 minutes
Total cooking time 1 hour
Serves 6

¹/2 quantity puff pastry (see page 60)
I egg, beaten

FILLING
30 g (I oz) unsalted butter
I onion, chopped
3 large spring onions, cut into thin
  2 cm (³/4 inch) sticks
190 g (6¹/4 oz) frozen English spinach, thawed
I egg
180 ml (5³/4 fl oz) thick (double) cream
250 g (8 oz) Brie, thinly sliced
2 ripe tomatoes, thinly sliced and dried
  on paper towels
2 tablespoons grated Parmesan

1 Grease an 18.5 x 2.5 cm (7¹/4 x 1 inch) loose-bottomed flan tin. Preheat the oven to moderately hot 200°C (400°F/Gas 6). Roll out the pastry on a lightly floured surface to a 1 mm (¹/16 inch) thickness, or as thinly as you can—thin enough to read through it—and line the prepared tin (see Chef's techniques, page 59).

2 Bake blind for 15–20 minutes, or until golden. Remove the beans and paper, return to the oven for 5 minutes, then brush the pastry case with the beaten egg (see Chef's techniques, page 59). Reduce the oven to moderate 180°C (350°F/Gas 4).

3 To make the filling, melt the butter in a frying pan. Add the onion and cook for about 3 minutes, or until soft. Add the spring onion, cook for 1 minute, then add the spinach. Season generously with salt and pepper, and stir until well mixed. Cook over high heat for about 7 minutes, or until the liquid has evaporated.

4 Whisk the egg and cream together in a bowl, and season with salt and pepper. Place the spinach mixture on the bottom of the pastry, cover with a layer of Brie and lay the tomato evenly on top. Pour the egg and cream mixture over the tomato and sprinkle the Parmesan over the top. Bake for about 25 minutes, or until set and golden. Set on a wire rack to cool slightly before removing from the tin. Serve the flan warm.

Fresh crab tartlets

These tartlets may be made to any size, depending on whether they are to be served as finger food, a first course, or as part of a buffet lunch or supper. The pastry cases, however, should not be filled too far in advance or the pastry will become soggy.

Preparation time **2 hours + 15 minutes chilling**
Total cooking time **15 minutes**
Makes 8

FILLING
I cucumber
1/2 teaspoon salt
I yellow capsicum (pepper)
2 tomatoes, peeled and seeded (see page 63)

1/2 quantity shortcrust pastry (see page 58)
250 g (8 oz) fresh crab meat
2 tablespoons chopped fresh chives

MAYONNAISE
I egg yolk
2 teaspoons Dijon mustard
125 ml (4 fl oz) oil

1 To make the filling, cut the ends from the cucumber and peel. Cut in half lengthways and scrape out the seeds using a teaspoon. Cut into very small dice, about 3 mm (1/8 inch). Toss with the salt. Trim the capsicum, remove the seeds, and dice the same size as the cucumber. Cut the tomatoes into dice the same size as the cucumber and capsicum, and drain on paper towels.
2 Preheat the oven to warm 170°C (325°F/Gas 3). Grease eight 7 x 1.5 cm (2 3/4 x 5/8 inch) tartlet tins. Roll out the pastry on a lightly floured surface to a thickness of 2 mm (1/8 inch). Refrigerate for 5 minutes. Using a 10 cm (4 inch) round cutter, cut out eight

rounds. Ease a pastry round into each tin, pressing well along the bottoms so that the dough extends slightly above the edges of the tins. Refrigerate for 10 minutes.
3 Trim the pastry to fit the tins. Lightly prick the base of the pastry with a fork, and bake blind for 8–10 minutes, or until the pastry colours slightly. Remove the beans and paper, and bake for a further 2–3 minutes, or until golden brown (see Chef's techniques, page 59). Leave the tartlets for 5 minutes before removing from the tins and placing on a wire rack to cool.
4 To make the mayonnaise, whisk the egg yolk and mustard in a deep bowl until smooth. Gradually whisk in the oil in a steady stream. Once all the oil has been incorporated, season to taste with salt and ground white pepper. Mix 3–4 tablespoons of the mayonnaise into the crab until the mixture holds together. Set aside.
5 Strain off the excess water from the cucumbers then drain on paper towels and pat dry. Place all the diced vegetables in a bowl and mix in 2–3 tablespoons of the mayonnaise until the mixture holds together. Divide the filling among the tartlet cases, then top with the crab. Spoon a little mayonnaise on top of each tart, and sprinkle with the chopped chives.

Chef's tips Each step can be prepared in advance but do not fill the tartlet shells until ready to serve. For a different flavour, mix a little curry powder into the vegetable mixture.

If using frozen or canned crab meat, remove excess water by placing in a clean tea towel and squeezing out all the liquid.

Tomato, basil and mozzarella quiche

A quiche with an Italian twist of flavours that is excellent served either warm or cold, making it ideal for picnics or lunch boxes.

Preparation time **30 minutes**
Total cooking time **1 hour 10 minutes**
Serves 6

[❋]

¹/₂ quantity shortcrust pastry (see page 58)

FILLING
2 eggs
50 ml (1³/₄ fl oz) milk
50 ml (1³/₄ fl oz) thick (double) cream
pinch of nutmeg, optional
pinch of cayenne, optional
2 small tomatoes, halved, seeded and cut into
  1 cm (¹/₂ inch) pieces
150 g (5 oz) mozzarella cheese, grated
1 tablespoon finely chopped fresh basil
  (see Chef's tip)

1 Preheat the oven to moderately hot 200°C (400°F/ Gas 6). Grease a 20.5 x 2.5 cm (8¹/₄ x 1 inch) loose-bottomed flan tin. Roll out the pastry on a lightly floured surface to a 3 mm (¹/₈ inch) thickness and line the prepared tin (see Chef's techniques, page 59).

2 Bake blind for 10–15 minutes, or until firm. Remove the beans and paper, and bake for another 10 minutes, or until dry and golden (see Chef's techniques, page 59). Remove from the oven to cool. Reduce the temperature of the oven to warm 170°C (325°F/Gas 3).

3 To make the filling, beat together the eggs, milk and cream in a bowl. Season with salt and pepper, adding the nutmeg and cayenne to taste, if using. Sprinkle the tomato, cheese and basil over the base of the flan. Pour in the egg mixture and bake for 35–45 minutes. Check from time to time to make sure that the filling is not bubbling. If it is bubbling, the oven is too hot and the temperature should be lowered. When cooked, the filling should be just firm to the touch and the surface golden brown. Set on a wire rack to cool slightly before removing from the tin. Serve warm or cold, accompanied by a crisp green salad.

Chef's tip The basil should be chopped just before using to prevent it from discolouring.

Mussel chaussons with garlic cream

A chausson, literally meaning slipper in French, is a pastry turnover, or semicircular shape,
made from a thin round of puff pastry folded over a filling. These are best served warm.

Preparation time **1 hour 10 minutes**
+ 25 minutes chilling
Total cooking time **50 minutes**
Serves 4

1/2 quantity puff pastry (see page 60)
I egg, beaten with a pinch of salt
3 sprigs fresh chervil, to garnish

FILLING
30 g (1 oz) unsalted butter
I carrot, cut into julienne strips (see Chef's tip)
100 g (31/4 oz) leek, white part only, cut into julienne
strips (see page 63)
I celery stick, cut into julienne strips
few drops of lemon juice
100 ml (31/4 fl oz) dry white wine
2 French shallots, finely chopped
I kg (2 lb) mussels, scrubbed and beards removed

GARLIC CREAM
10 cloves garlic
300 ml (10 fl oz) thick (double) cream

1 Roll out the pastry on a lightly floured surface to a
3 mm (1/8 inch) thickness. Cut out eight circles with a
12 cm (5 inch) plain round cutter. Place on a tray and
refrigerate for at least 10 minutes. Lightly grease a
baking tray with melted butter and chill until needed.
2 To make the filling, melt the butter in a shallow pan
and add the carrot, leek and celery. Season lightly with
salt and pepper. Cover and cook over low heat for
6–10 minutes, or until soft and transparent. Add lemon
juice to taste, and cool.
3 Put the wine and shallots in a pan and add the
mussels, checking to ensure they are closed. Discard any

that remain open as you handle them. Cover the pan,
bring to the boil and simmer for about 5 minutes, or
until all the mussels have opened. Discard any that have
not opened. Drain and reserve the liquid. Reserve eight
mussels in their shells. Remove the remaining mussels
from their shells and leave to cool.

4 Place the pastry on a lightly floured surface. Brush a
1 cm (1/2 inch) border of beaten egg around the top
edge of each circle. Cover half of each circle, within the
limit of the egg, with the vegetables and shelled mussels.
Turn the unfilled side over to form a semicircle and
press the edge with the back of a fork to seal. Make two
small cuts on the top with the point of a small sharp
knife to allow the steam to escape during baking. Use
the knife point to score pattern marks, crisscross or
pinwheel, but do not cut through the pastry. Sprinkle a
few drops of water on the prepared baking tray and
place the turnovers on the tray. Brush their surface, but
not the cut edges, with the beaten egg, and refrigerate
for 15 minutes. Preheat the oven to hot 220°C (425°F/
Gas 7). Brush again with beaten egg. Bake for 5 minutes,
then reduce the heat to moderately hot 200°C
(400°F/Gas 6) and bake for 10–15 minutes, or until the
turnovers are well risen, crisp and golden brown.
5 To make the garlic cream, put the garlic in a small
pan, cover with cold water and bring to the boil. Drain
and repeat once more. Return the garlic to the pan, add
the cream and 100 ml (31/4 fl oz) of the mussel cooking
liquid, cover and simmer gently for 15 minutes, or until
the garlic is soft. Pour into a blender or food processor,
and process until smooth. Season with salt and pepper.
6 To serve, spoon the hot garlic cream over the base of
four warm plates, set the hot turnovers on top and
garnish with the reserved mussels and sprigs of chervil.

Chef's tip Julienne strips are even-sized strips of
vegetables, the size and shape of matchsticks.

Cheese tart

The Dijon mustard added to this delicious rich tart filling gives the cheese flavour a good 'lift'.
If desired, a small amount of cayenne pepper could also be added.

*Preparation time **20 minutes***
*Total cooking time **50 minutes***

Serves 6

☼

1/2 quantity shortcrust pastry (see page 58)

FILLING
150 g (5 oz) Gruyère cheese, grated
3 eggs
200 ml (6¹/2 fl oz) thick (double) cream
pinch of nutmeg
1/4 teaspoon Dijon mustard

1 Preheat the oven to moderate 180°C (350°F/Gas 4). Grease a 20.5 x 2.5 cm (8¹/4 x 1 inch) loose-bottomed flan tin. Roll out the shortcrust pastry on a lightly floured surface to a circle about 3 mm (¹/8 inch) thick and line the prepared tin (see Chef's techniques, page 59).

2 Bake blind for 10 minutes, or until firm. Remove the beans and paper, and bake for another 5–10 minutes, or until the centre begins to colour (see Chef's techniques, page 59). Remove from the oven to cool.

3 Sprinkle the cheese over the base of the pastry. Whisk together the eggs, cream, nutmeg and mustard, and season with salt and pepper. Pour the mixture over the cheese and bake for 20–30 minutes, or until the mixture is set and golden brown. Set on a wire rack to cool slightly before removing from the tin.

4 Serve the tart warm or cold with a green salad and tomatoes for a light summer lunch.

Scrambled egg and smoked salmon tartlets

Add a touch of sophistication to brunch by serving these elegant tartlets instead of scrambled eggs on toast. For a truly creamy result it is vital not to overcook the eggs.

Preparation time **20 minutes**
Total cooking time **20 minutes**
Makes **6**

1/2 quantity shortcrust pastry (see page 58)
6 sprigs fresh chervil, to garnish

FILLING
20 g (3/4 oz) unsalted butter
6 eggs
90 ml (3 fl oz) thick (double) cream
100 g (31/4 oz) smoked salmon, cut into thin strips
2 teaspoons caviar, to garnish

1 Preheat the oven to moderately hot 200°C (400°F/ Gas 6). Grease six 7 x 1.5 cm (23/4 x 5/8 inch) tartlet tins. Roll out the pastry on a lightly floured surface to a circle approximately 2 mm (1/8 inch) thick. Cut out six circles with a 13 cm (5 inch) plain round pastry cutter, and use them to line the prepared tins (see Chef's techniques, page 59).

2 Bake blind for about 7 minutes, or until firm. Remove the beans and paper, and bake for another 3–5 minutes, or until the centre is golden (see Chef's techniques, page 59). Remove the tartlets from the tins and keep warm.

3 To make the filling, heat the butter in a pan over low to medium heat. Whisk the eggs lightly with the cream, and pour into the pan. Cook the eggs, over low heat, stirring with a wooden spoon to scrape the egg from the base of the pan, until just setting but still very creamy in consistency. Remove from the heat and stir in half the smoked salmon until well combined.

4 Fill the warm pastry tartlets immediately with the egg mixture. Decorate each with the remaining smoked salmon and a little caviar, and garnish with a small sprig of chervil. Serve warm.

Chef's tip Always remove the pan from the heat while the scrambled egg is just creamy. The pan is hot and the egg will continue to cook as you serve it. When overcooked, the eggs will be tough and water will begin to run from them.

Chèvre and watercress quiche

The rather peppery flavour of the watercress complements the creamy goats' cheese filling in this recipe. This quiche could also be made as individual tartlets and served either warm or cold.

*Preparation time **30 minutes***
*Total cooking time **1 hour 15 minutes***
Serves 4–6

FILLING
250 g (8 oz) watercress
3 eggs
100 ml (3 1/4 fl oz) thick (double) cream
nutmeg, to taste
150 g (5 oz) chèvre (goats' cheese), cut into
  1.5 cm (5/8 inch) slices

1/2 quantity shortcrust pastry (see page 58)
I egg, beaten

1 To make the filling, remove the large stems from the watercress, rinse and pat dry with paper towels. Bring 2 litres water to the boil, add some salt and cook the watercress for 10 seconds. Drain, refresh in iced water for 3 minutes, then drain again (see Chef's techniques, page 63). Squeeze out any excess water, then coarsely chop the watercress. Season with salt and pepper.

2 Preheat the oven to moderate 180°C (350°F/Gas 4). Lightly grease a 20.5 x 2.5 cm (8 1/4 x 1 inch) loose-bottomed flan tin. Roll out the dough on a lightly floured surface to a thickness of 3 mm (1/8 inch) and line the prepared tin (see Chef's techniques, page 59). Bake blind for about 25 minutes, or until firm. Remove the beans and paper, and brush the bottom of the pastry with the beaten egg. Bake for another 7 minutes (see Chef's techniques, page 59).

3 Whisk the eggs with the cream, and season with nutmeg, salt and pepper. Sprinkle the bottom of the tart with the chopped watercress, and arrange the slices of chèvre on top. Add the egg mixture and bake for 30–40 minutes, or until set and a knife inserted into the centre comes out clean. Set on a wire rack to cool slightly before removing from the tin. Leave for 5 minutes before cutting.

Anchovy sticks

Anchovy sticks, with light crisp pastry and salty anchovies, are delicious served with wine and champagne, hence their popularity at cocktail parties.

*Preparation time **20 minutes + 30 minutes chilling***
*Total cooking time **10 minutes***
Makes about 80

¹/₂ quantity puff pastry (see page 60) or 250 g (8 oz)
puff pastry trimmings
1 egg, beaten
20–25 anchovy fillets

1 Lightly dust a 30 x 45 cm (12 x 18 inch) baking tray with flour. Roll out the pastry on a lightly floured surface to a rectangle the approximate size of the baking tray. The pastry should be rolled out as thinly as possible—thin enough to read through. Carefully lift the pastry onto the baking tray, cover with plastic wrap and refrigerate for 20 minutes.

2 Preheat the oven to moderately hot 200°C (400°F/ Gas 6). Cut the pastry in half lengthways and carefully transfer to a lightly floured work surface. Brush one of the strips with some beaten egg. Lay the anchovy fillets across the egg-brushed pastry at approximately 2.5 cm (1 inch) intervals. Lay the remaining strip of pastry over the top and roll lightly with the rolling pin to press the layers together. Cut the pastry lengthways, at 1 cm (¹/₂ inch) intervals, to form long strips, then cut across the strips to form sticks approximately 7 cm (2³/₄ inches) long. Refrigerate for 10 minutes.

3 Place the anchovy sticks on two lightly greased baking trays, and brush with the beaten egg. Bake for approximately 8–10 minutes, or until they are puffed and golden brown. Serve warm or cold.

Leek and Brie flamiche

The flamiche derives its name from the Flemish word for cake, as originally it was in fact a type of cake made from bread dough and served with butter. Nowadays, however, it usually refers to a pie filled with vegetables or cheese, or both, as in this particular recipe.

Preparation time **1 hour 5 minutes**
  + 30 minutes chilling
Total cooking time **55 minutes**
Serves **4–6**

❋ ❋

PASTRY
250 g (8 oz) plain flour
1 teaspoon salt
60 g (2 oz) unsalted butter
1 egg
1 egg yolk

1 egg, beaten

FILLING
60 g (2 oz) unsalted butter, cubed
400 g (12 3/4 oz) leek, white part only, thinly sliced (see page 63)
150 g (5 oz) Brie
1 egg
1 egg yolk
50 ml (1 3/4 fl oz) thick (double) cream

1 To make the pastry, sift the flour and salt together into a bowl. Using your fingertips, rub in the butter until the mixture resembles fine breadcrumbs. Make a well in the centre and add the egg, egg yolk and 2 1/2 tablespoons water. Mix well, form into a ball and refrigerate for 20 minutes, wrapped in plastic wrap.

2 To make the filling, melt the butter in a deep frying pan and slowly cook the leek, covered, for 5 minutes. Cook for a further 5 minutes, uncovered, or until all the liquid has evaporated, being careful not to allow the leek to brown. Transfer the leek to a colander and set aside to cool.

3 Preheat the oven to warm 170°C (325°F/Gas 3). Lightly grease a 20.5 x 2.5 cm (8 1/4 x 1 inch) loose-bottomed flan tin. Divide the pastry in half and roll out one half on a lightly floured surface to a thickness of 3 mm (1/8 inch) and line the prepared tin (see Chef's techniques, page 59), leaving a 1 cm (1/2 inch) overhang. Roll out the second piece of dough on a lightly floured surface to a 22.5 cm (8 3/4 inch) circle, and refrigerate until needed.

4 Remove the rind of the cheese and cut the cheese into small cubes. Spread the leek over the bottom of the pastry, and sprinkle with the cheese. Whisk together the egg, egg yolk and cream. Pour over the leek and cheese. Brush the edge of the pastry with the beaten egg and place the second piece of pastry on top. Trim the top pastry sheet so that it is even with the lower sheet. Pinch the dough well to seal the two pieces together, and trim the edges by pressing down with the thumb against the edge of the tin. Brush the top with the egg and refrigerate for 10 minutes. Brush again with the beaten egg and cut a hole in the centre using a small round cutter. Bake for 40–45 minutes, or until golden. Set on a wire rack to cool slightly before removing from the tin. Leave for 5 minutes before cutting.

Asparagus feuilletés with chive butter sauce

Feuilletés are puff pastry cases that are generally filled with meat, vegetables or seafood.
They can be either square, rectangular, triangular or diamond shaped. In this recipe they are filled
with asparagus and Brie, and served with a mouthwatering chive butter sauce.

Preparation time **20 minutes + 20 minutes chilling**
Total cooking time **25 minutes**

Makes 8

FILLING
16 fresh asparagus tips, about 6 cm (2¹/₂ inches) long
80 g (2³/₄ oz) Brie, cut into 8 slices

¹/₂ quantity puff pastry (see page 60)
1 egg, beaten

CHIVE BUTTER SAUCE
150 g (5 oz) unsalted butter, chilled and cubed
1 teaspoon lemon juice
2 tablespoons chopped fresh chives

1 To make the filling, bring a pan of salted water to the boil, add the asparagus tips and cook for 2–3 minutes, or until tender. Drain the asparagus, refresh in iced water for 5 minutes, drain again, then transfer to a tray to cool (see Chef's techniques, page 63).

2 Roll out the pastry on a lightly floured surface to a 21 x 26 cm (8¹/₂ x 10¹/₂ inch) rectangle, approximately 5 mm (¹/₄ inch) thick. Trim the two long sides to straighten them, and cut the pastry into eight 7 cm (2³/₄ inch) diamonds or squares. Place slightly apart on a damp baking tray and refrigerate for 20 minutes.

3 Preheat the oven to moderately hot 200°C (400°F/Gas 6). Brush the top surface of the pastry with beaten egg. Do not brush the side edges as the egg will set and prevent the pastry from rising. Lightly score the top of the pastry in a crisscross pattern with a thin knife. Bake for approximately 15 minutes, or until well risen, crisp and golden brown. Split in half horizontally with a sharp knife, and scrape out any soft dough. Place a slice of Brie in the pastry cases and top with the asparagus so that the tips are just protruding. Replace the pastry lid and keep warm in a warm 160°C (315°F/Gas 2–3) oven.

4 To make the sauce, bring 100 ml (3¹/₄ fl oz) water to the boil in a saucepan. Reduce the heat and whisk in the butter, a few pieces at a time, until the butter is well incorporated and the sauce is thickened. Season with salt and pepper, and stir in the lemon juice and chives.

5 To serve, spoon a little of the chive sauce into each pastry case and drizzle some of the sauce onto the plate. Serve warm.

Chef's tip Any leftover puff pastry can be used to make anchovy sticks (see page 49).

Seafood quiche

*The filling for this lovely seafood quiche is extemely quick and simple to prepare
as the seafood may be purchased precooked.*

Preparation time **35 minutes**
Total cooking time **1 hour 10 minutes**
Serves 4–6

❄

1/2 quantity shortcrust pastry (see page 58)
I egg, beaten

FILLING
200 g (6¹/2 oz) cooked shelled small prawns
170 g (5¹/2 oz) cooked crab meat
3 eggs
250 ml (8 fl oz) thick (double) cream
nutmeg, to taste
40 g (1¹/4 oz) Gruyère cheese, grated

1 Preheat the oven to warm 170°C (325°F/Gas 3).
Lightly grease a 22 x 3.5 cm (8³/4 x 1¹/4 inch) loose-
bottomed flan tin. Roll out the pastry on a lightly
floured surface to a thickness of 3 mm (¹/8 inch) and
line the prepared tin (see Chef's techniques, page 59).
Bake blind for about 25 minutes, or until firm. Remove
the beans and paper, and brush the bottom of the pastry
with the beaten egg. Bake for another 3 minutes (see
Chef's techniques, page 59).

2 To make the filling, drain any excess water or juice
from the seafood and place on paper towels. Whisk the
eggs, cream and nutmeg together. Season with salt and
freshly ground pepper.

3 Sprinkle the crab and seafood over the bottom of the
pastry shell. Pour in the egg mixture, sprinkle with the
grated cheese and bake for 35–40 minutes, or until the
top is golden brown and a knife inserted into the centre
comes out clean. Set on a wire rack to cool slightly
before removing from the tin. Leave for 5 minutes
before cutting.

Ham gougères

Traditionally a gougère is a round or ring-shaped cheese choux pastry. This variation uses plain choux pastry and a sprinkling of cheese to make small puffs that are then filled with a creamy smoked-ham and cheese sauce.

*Preparation time **30 minutes***
*Total cooking time **25 minutes***
Serves 6

1 quantity choux pastry (see page 62)
1 egg, beaten with a pinch of salt
1 tablespoon Gruyère or Parmesan cheese, grated

FILLING
30 g (1 oz) unsalted butter
30 g (1 oz) plain flour
250 ml (8 fl oz) milk
50 g (1 3/4 oz) Gruyère cheese, grated
100 g (3 1/4 oz) smoked ham, finely diced
1 teaspoon English mustard
pinch of cayenne pepper
pinch of white pepper

1 Grease a baking tray and refrigerate until needed. Preheat the oven to moderately hot 200°C (400°F/ Gas 6). Spoon the pastry into a piping bag fitted with a 1 cm (1/2 inch) plain nozzle. Pipe 12 rounds of pastry onto the prepared baking tray, approximately 1 cm (1/2 inch) at the base and 1.5 cm (5/8 inch) high. Brush the pastry with the beaten egg, and sprinkle with the grated cheese. Bake for about 20 minutes, or until golden brown all over. Once baked, leave the choux buns to cool in the oven with the heat turned off and the oven door open. This will help dry out the inside of the pastry.

2 To make the filling, melt the butter in a heavy-based pan over low to medium heat. Sprinkle the flour over the base of the pan and cook for 1–2 minutes without browning, stirring continuously with a wooden spoon. Slowly add the milk to the flour mixture, whisking vigorously to prevent lumps forming. Bring to the boil over medium heat, then simmer for 3–4 minutes. If the sauce has lumps, pass it through a fine sieve and reheat in a clean pan. Stir in the cheese, smoked ham and mustard. Season to taste with salt, cayenne and white pepper.

3 Spoon the filling into a piping bag fitted with a small round nozzle. Using the tip of a small knife, make a hole in the bottom of each choux bun. Place the tip of the piping bag into the hole and fill with the cheese mixture. Repeat with all the choux buns. Serve warm with a salad, allowing two per person.

Chef's techniques

♦

Shortcrust pastry

This delicious dough produces one of the most versatile pastries for quiches and tarts, and is also one of the easiest to make.

Preparation time **10 minutes + 20 minutes chilling**
Total cooking time **Nil**
Makes **530 g (1 lb 1 oz)**

200 g (6¹/2 oz) plain flour
large pinch of salt
100 g (3¹/4 oz) unsalted butter, chilled
1 egg, lightly beaten
2–3 teaspoons water

1 In a large bowl, sift together the flour and salt. Cut the butter into small 1 cm (1/2 inch) cubes and place in the flour.

2 Rub the butter into the flour using your fingertips until the mixture resembles fine breadcrumbs.

3 Make a well in the centre and pour in the combined egg and water.

4 Slowly work the mixture together with a palette knife or pastry scraper until it forms a rough ball. If it is slightly sticky, add a little more flour. Turn out onto a lightly floured cool surface and knead very gently until just smooth (no more than 20 seconds). Wrap the pastry in plastic wrap and chill for at least 20 minutes before using.

Chef's tip This quantity of pastry is sufficient to line two shallow 18–20 cm (7–8 inch) flan tins. If only making one flan or tart, divide the pastry into two and wrap separately in plastic wrap. Use one piece and put the second one in a plastic bag and seal, airtight, to freeze and use on another occasion.

Put the cubes of butter in the flour and salt, and rub into the dry ingredients.

Continue rubbing the butter into the flour until the mixture resembles fine breadcrumbs.

Pour the combined egg and water into the well.

Slowly work the mixture together with a palette knife until it forms a rough ball.

Lining a flan tin

Be very careful when handling the dough to avoid stretching it.

Place the dough over a rolling pin and unroll loosely over the tin.

Press the sides of the pastry into the flutes or sides of the tin by using a small ball of excess pastry.

Use a rolling pin to trim the pastry edges. Gently but firmly roll across the top of the tin. Refrigerate for 10 minutes.

Prick the pastry shell with a fork to allow steam to escape during baking.

Baking blind

Baking the pastry before adding the filling prevents the base becoming soggy during cooking.

Crush a sheet of greaseproof paper lightly into a ball. Open out the paper, then lay it inside the pastry shell.

Spread a layer of baking beans or rice over the paper, then press down gently so that the beans or rice and the paper rest firmly against the sides of the flan.

Bake according to the time specified in the recipe, or until firm. Remove the beans or rice and paper.

If indicated in the recipe, rebake until the pastry looks dry and is evenly coloured.

Puff pastry

This pastry requires more effort and time than the other pastries, but the result is a lovely buttery and flaky base for any tart or pastry. If you are short of time, bought sheets or blocks of puff are a good alternative.

*Preparation time **1 day***
*Total cooking time **Nil***
Makes 530 g (1 lb 1 oz)

DOUGH BASE
250 g (8 oz) strong or plain flour
1 teaspoon salt
2–3 drops of lemon juice
125 ml (4 fl oz) water,
40 g (1¹/4 oz) unsalted butter, melted

100 g (3¹/4 oz) unsalted butter, chilled

1 To make the dough base, sift the flour and salt onto a cool work surface and make a well in the centre. Add the lemon juice to the water, then place in the well with the butter and mix together with your fingertips. With the side of a palette knife or a pastry scraper, use a cutting action to draw in the flour and work it into the butter mixture until the dry flour disappears and the mixture resembles loose crumbs. Draw together with your hands and knead lightly, adding a few drops of water if necessary, to form a smooth soft ball of dough.
2 Cut an 'X' on top of the dough to prevent shrinkage, then wrap in lightly floured greaseproof paper or plastic wrap. Chill for 1 hour in the refrigerator—this will make the dough more pliable for rolling. Place the chilled butter between two pieces of greaseproof paper or plastic wrap. Tap it with the side of a rolling pin and shape into a 2 cm (3/4 inch) thick square. This action will make the butter pliable to roll, without melting it.
3 Unwrap the dough and place it on a lightly floured cool surface. Roll the dough from just off centre to form a cross shape with a mound in the centre.
4 Place the butter on the central mound and fold over the four sides of the dough to enclose it completely.

Sift the flour and salt onto a work surface and make a well in the centre. Add the lemon juice, water and butter and blend together with your fingertips.

Cut an 'X' on top of the pastry with a sharp knife.

Unwrap the chilled dough and place it on a lightly floured surface. Roll from just off centre to form a cross shape with a mound in the centre.

Place the butter on the central mound and fold over the four sides of the dough to enclose it.

5 Roll over the top and bottom of the dough to seal the edges. On a lightly floured surface, roll the dough into a 12 x 35 cm (5 x 14 inch) rectangle.

6 Fold in three by folding the bottom third up towards the middle and the top third down. Brush off the excess flour and ensure that the edges all meet neatly. Make an indentation with your finger to record the first roll and fold. Wrap in plastic wrap and chill for 30 minutes.

7 Give the dough a quarter turn with the folded side on your left as if it was a book. With a rolling pin, gently press down to seal the edges.

8 Repeat steps 5–7 three more times, remembering to record each roll with an indentation and chilling for 30 minutes after each roll. After two rolls and folds, you should have two indentations. The finished pastry should have four indentations, and will start to look smoother as you continue to roll and fold. Leave the dough to rest in the refrigerator for a final 30 minutes. The puff pastry is now ready to use. It can be frozen whole, or cut into smaller portions, then used as needed.

Chef's tips When making puff pastry, work on a cool surface to prevent the butter from melting and forming a heavy dough. In hot weather, it may be necessary to refrigerate the dough for an extra 15 minutes during the final resting.

Making puff pastry is not difficult, but it is time consuming, so make two or three quantities at once and freeze the extra. Thaw the pastry by leaving it overnight in the refrigerator. Puff will keep in the refrigerator for 4 days and in the freezer for 3 months.

Seal the edges of the dough by pressing down with a rolling pin. Roll the pastry into a rectangle.

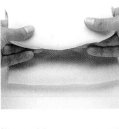

Fold the dough in three by folding the bottom third up towards the middle and the top third down.

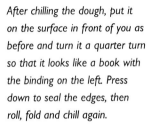

After chilling the dough, put it on the surface in front of you as before and turn it a quarter turn so that it looks like a book with the binding on the left. Press down to seal the edges, then roll, fold and chill again.

Continue rolling, folding and chilling, trying to maintain an even finish and neat corners.

Choux pastry

This pastry is cooked twice to give the lightness found in éclairs and choux buns. Before the final cooking, the paste is fairly wet and needs to be piped.

Preparation time **5 minutes**
Total cooking time **10–15 minutes**

60 g (2 oz) plain flour
125 ml (4 fl oz) water
50 g (1³⁄4 oz) unsalted butter, cubed
pinch of salt
pinch of sugar
2 eggs

1 Sift the flour onto a sheet of greaseproof paper. Place the water, butter, salt and sugar in a pan. Heat until the butter and water come to the boil. Remove from the heat and add the flour all at once.

2 Mix well using a wooden spoon. Return to the heat and mix until a smooth ball forms and the paste leaves the sides of the pan.

3 Remove from the heat and place the paste in a bowl. Lightly beat the eggs in a small bowl. Using a wooden spoon or electric beaters, add the eggs to the paste a little at a time, beating well after each addition.

4 The mixture is ready to use when it is smooth, thick and glossy.

Chef's tips It is essential when making choux to measure the ingredients carefully, as too much moisture can cause the choux to collapse. Traditionally, bakers weigh the eggs in order to determine the weight of the dry ingredients.

Don't be fooled by golden coloured choux! If the cracks of the choux are still light yellow or much lighter than the rest of the choux, this indicates that the interior is not quite cooked. Reduce the temperature to warm 160°C (315°F/Gas 2–3) and continue baking.

Once boiling, remove from the heat and immediately stir in the sifted flour.

Return the pan to the heat and cook until the mixture forms a smooth ball that comes away from the sides of the pan.

Remove from the heat and transfer the mixture to a bowl. Gradually beat in the eggs with a wooden spoon.

The mixture is ready to use when it is smooth, thick and glossy.

Grilling capsicums

Grilling capsicums allows you to remove their skins and produces a delicious sweet flavour.

Preheat a grill. Cut the capsicums in half and remove the seeds and membrane.

Grill the capsicums until the skin blisters and blackens. Place in a plastic bag and allow to cool. When cool, peel off the skin.

Refreshing vegetables

The process of refreshing helps retain the vibrant colour of blanched vegetables.

Cook the vegetables in boiling water until tender.

Drain, and plunge into a bowl of iced water to stop the cooking process and refresh the vegetables. Drain.

Preparing tomatoes

Many recipes call for peeled, seeded tomatoes. It is an easy process if you follow these instructions.

Using a very sharp knife, score a small cross in the base of each tomato.

Blanch the tomatoes in a large pan of boiling water for 10 seconds. Remove and plunge into a bowl of ice-cold water to stop the cooking and keep the flesh firm.

Pull away the skin from the cross, and discard the skins. If a recipe calls for the removal of the tomato seeds, cut the tomato in half and use a teaspoon to gently scoop out the seeds.

Washing leeks

Leeks are often used in cooking as they impart a unique flavour.

Before use, leeks need to be rinsed thoroughly under cold running water to dislodge and remove all traces of dirt or grit. Slit the green tops to help the water run through the tightly furled leaves.

Published in 1998 by Merehurst Limited, Ferry House, 51–57 Lacy Road, Putney, London SW15 1PR.

Merehurst Limited, Murdoch Books and Le Cordon Bleu thank the 32 masterchefs of all the Le Cordon Bleu Schools, whose knowledge and expertise have made this book possible, especially: Chef Cliche (MOF), Chef Terrien, Chef Boucheret, Chef Duchêne (MOF), Chef Guillut, Chef Steneck, Paris; Chef Males, Chef Walsh, Chef Hardy, London; Chef Chantefort, Chef Bertin, Chef Jambert, Chef Honda, Tokyo; Chef Salembien, Chef Boutin, Chef Harris, Sydney; Chef Lawes, Adelaide; Chef Guiet, Chef Denis, Ottawa. Of the many students who helped the Chefs test each recipe, a special mention to graduates David Welch and Allen Wertheim. A very special acknowledgment to Directors Susan Eckstein, Great Britain, and Kathy Shaw, Paris, who have been responsible for the coordination of the Le Cordon Bleu team throughout this series.

Managing Editor: Kay Halsey
Series Concept, Design and Art Direction: Juliet Cohen
Editor: Justine Upex
Food Director: Jody Vassallo
Food Editors: Roslyn Anderson, Tracy Rutherford
Designer: Norman Baptista
Photographer: Damian Webber
Food Stylist: Marie-Hélène Clauzon
Food Preparation: Christine Sheppard
Chef's Techniques Photographer: Reg Morrison
Home Economists: Michelle Lawton, Kerrie Mullins, Justine Poole, Kerrie Ray

Creative Director: Marylouise Brammer
International Sales Director: Mark Newman
CEO & Publisher: Anne Wilson

ISBN 1 85391 770 2

Printed by Toppan Printing (S) Pte Ltd
First Printed 1998
©Design and photography Murdoch Books® 1998
©Text Le Cordon Bleu 1998

A catalogue record for this book is available from the British Library.

Distributed in the UK by D Services, 6 Euston Street, Freemen's Common, Leicester LE2 7SS Tel 0116-254-7671 Fax 0116-254-4670.
Distributed in Canada by Whitecap (Vancouver) Ltd, 351 Lynn Avenue, North Vancouver, BC V7J 2C4
Tel 604-980-9852 Fax 604-980-8197 or Whitecap (Ontario) Ltd, 47 Coldwater Road, North York, ON M3B 1Y8
Tel 416-444-3442 Fax 416-444-6630
Published and distributed in Australia by Murdoch Books®, 45 Jones Street, Ultimo NSW 2007

The Publisher and Le Cordon Bleu wish to thank Carole Sweetnam for her help with this series.
Front cover: Spinach and ricotta quiche.

IMPORTANT INFORMATION

CONVERSION GUIDE

1 cup = 250 ml (8 fl oz)
1 Australian tablespoon = 20 ml (4 teaspoons)
1 UK tablespoon = 15 ml (3 teaspoons)

NOTE: We have used 20 ml tablespoons. If you are using a 15 ml tablespoon, for most recipes the difference will be negligible. For recipes using baking powder, gelatine, bicarbonate of soda and flour, add an extra teaspoon for each tablespoon specified.

CUP CONVERSIONS—DRY INGREDIENTS

1 cup flour, plain or self-raising = 125 g (4 oz)
1 cup sugar, caster = 250 g (8 oz)
1 cup breadcrumbs, dry = 125 g (4 oz)

IMPORTANT: Those who might be at risk from the effects of salmonella food poisoning (the elderly, pregnant women, young children and those suffering from immune deficiency diseases) should consult their GP with any concerns about eating raw eggs.